TRAIL BLAZERS LEGENDS ALPHABET

Words by Robin Feiner

A is for **A**rvydas Sabonis. Fans waited nine years for this giant center to suit up for the Trail Blazers after they drafted him 24th overall in 1986. Arriving past his prime and riddled with injuries, this nimble Lithuanian legend's patented no-look and behind-the-back passes led to plenty of Portland baskets.

B is for Buck Williams. He brought a blue-collar attitude and interior toughness that elevated the Blazers to true title contenders when he arrived in 1989. With the ferocious Williams on the floor, there were no free trips down the lane, and rebounds turned into dogfights.

C is for **Cliff** Robinson. Uncle Cliffy entered the NBA with questions about his attitude, but he answered them during his 1989–97 Blazers career. The 1992–93 Sixth Man of the Year, Robinson helped lead the Blazers to two Finals, played in a team-record 461 consecutive games, and is sixth in franchise scoring.

D is for **D**amian Lillard. It's Dame Time. A legendary leader, Lillard earned seven All-Star selections in his first 11 seasons and is the Blazers' all-time leading scorer. His clutch playoff-series-winning threes against the Thunder and Rockets are two of the greatest moments in Portland hoops history.

E is for **E**van Turner. Despite fans' frustration over the size of his contract, Turner did a bit of everything on offense and grew into a great teammate during his 2016–19 stay in Portland. His legendary sense of humor made him a favorite amongst fans and fellow players.

Ff

F is for Enes **F**reedom.
Known as Enes Kanter when
he joined Portland late in the
2018–19 season, this big man
quickly made a big impact.
Admirably stepping into a
starting role, he helped the
Blazers make a legendary
Western Conference Finals
run for the first time in
18 years.

G is for Clyde 'The **G**lide' Drexler. Arguably the greatest Blazer, his legendary quickness, power, and confidence earned him eight All-Star nods in Portland from 1983–94. A high-flying Hall of Famer, Drexler took Portland to two Finals and left as the team's scoring, rebounds, and steals leader.

H is for Lionel **H**ollins.
This point guard was the
spark plug of coach Jack
Ramsay's legendary motion
offense that helped Portland
win the 1977 title. The L-Train
did it all, from bringing it on
defense every night to scoring
on the break and enabling
Bill Walton's post dominance.

I is for **I**ron Man.
This is the nickname for Wesley Matthews, whose legendary willingness to play through injuries – and 3-and-D skills – made him a crucial Blazer from 2010–15. He did his part even when he couldn't play, including firing up the crowd with an Iron Man mask in the 2015 playoffs.

Jj

J is for C.J. McCollum.
He formed a legendary
backcourt duo with Dame,
that lit it up on offense.
McCollum averaged
19 points per game in his
nine seasons in Portland
from 2013–2022, leaving
as the team's fifth-highest
scorer of all time.

K is for Jerome **K**ersey. Mr. Hustle's legendary physicality and determination made him a late-'80s and early-'90s Blazers legend. Many thought Kersey wouldn't make it in the NBA. But he ground his way from bit player to a starter, doing the dirty work while Clyde Drexler and Terry Porter did the scoring.

L is for **L**aMarcus Aldridge. Aldridge was a monster in the post, shooting his high-release jumper over just about anybody. Although overshadowed by Dame's heroics, LMA's legendary skills were on display in the first round of the 2014 playoffs, when he averaged 26 points and 11 rebounds.

M is for **M**aurice Lucas. Many credit The Enforcer's spirit and refusal to back down for turning the tide of the 1977 NBA Finals. The big man lives on through the team's annual Maurice Lucas Award, which goes to the player who displays the guard's legendary attitude on and off the court.

N is for Lloyd **N**eal. Reliable and rugged, Neal was the ultimate team player and the first Blazer number retired. This legend played his entire injury-shortened 1972–79 career with Portland, constantly adapting to different roles to fill in the gaps and helping win the 1977 title.

Oo

**O is for Greg Oden.
After picking Sam Bowie
over Michael Jordan in the
1984 Draft, the Blazers made
another legendary mistake
in 2007 by drafting Oden
first overall instead of Kevin
Durant. Oden missed four
of the next six seasons with
knee injuries, while Durant
became an all-time great.**

45

P is for Geoff **P**etrie.
Known as The Original
Trail Blazer, Petrie became
Portland's first-ever draft
pick in 1970. That season he
also became the team's first
All-Star and was Co-Rookie
of the Year. Unfortunately,
the legendary scorer's left
knee limited his career to
just six seasons.

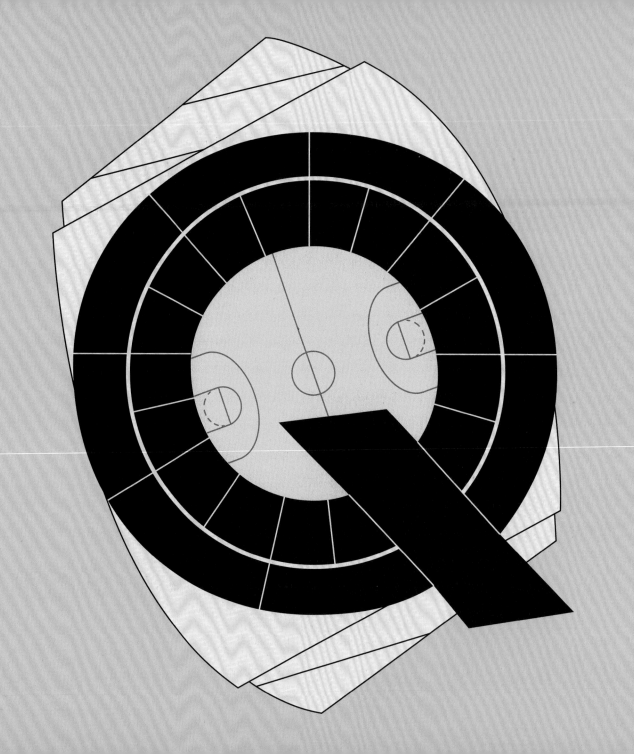

Q is for the Rose **Q**uarter. This entertainment district is where fans go to watch Blazers home games at the Moda Center, which was originally called the Rose Garden when it opened in 1995. It's hosted tons of legendary moments from Damian Lillard and C.J. McCollum, Brandon Roy, LaMarcus Aldridge, and many more.

R is for Brandon **R**oy.
An All-Star in three of his first four seasons, the 2006–07 Rookie of the Year was heading toward a legendary Blazers career. But Roy, the team's leader after the tough Jail Blazers era, was cut down by injury and out of the league by 2013.

**S is for 'Sheed.
Rasheed Wallace was
known for his legendary
unpredictability, signature
headband, and great
skill – not for being a hard
worker. Though he set
records for technical fouls,
he led the Blazers to the
playoffs in each of his
eight seasons in Portland
from 1996–2003.**

T is for **T**erry Porter. This point guard played his first 10 seasons in Portland from 1985–95, leaving as the franchise leader in threes and assists and second in points and steals. A deep threat, Porter formed a legendary duo with rim-attacking co-star Clyde Drexler that took the Blazers to two NBA Finals.

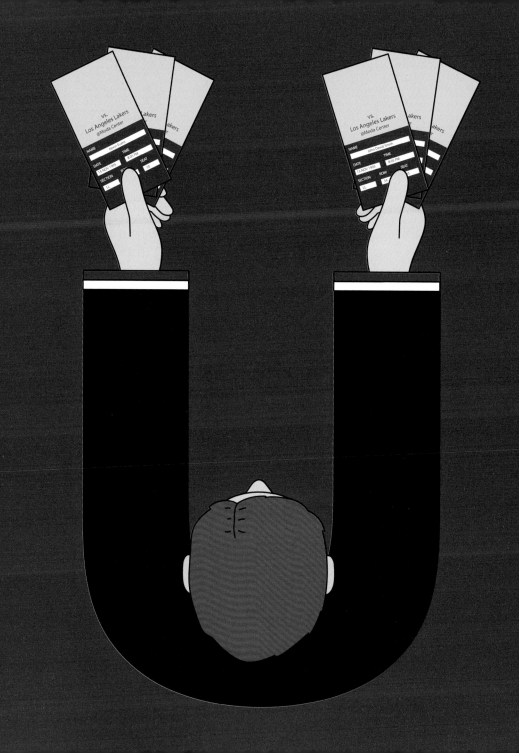

U is for **U**navailable tickets. Blazers fans are considered some of the best in the NBA. And that's perhaps best showcased by a legendary streak of 814 straight sellouts from 1977–95. That is believed to have been a U.S. professional sports record until 2011.

Vv

V is for Kiki **V**andeweghe. His legendary 47-point debut with the Blazers in 1984 showed fans just what this high-scoring forward could do. Though he dealt with an injured back during his five Rip City seasons, Vandeweghe's lightning-quick first step helped him set team scoring records.

W is for Bill **W**alton. He was the 1977 Finals MVP and the 1977–78 MVP when the Blazers started 50–10. But then this legendary center injured his foot twice – legendary breaks of the game. He was mad at team doctors and sat out the next season before being traded. A potential dynasty ended before it could start.

X is for Jim Pa**x**son. This guard repaid coach Jack Ramsay's faith in him by becoming the first Blazer to score 10,000 points. Paxson's legendary motor made it hard for defenders to keep up with him. He was a two-time All-Star in his eight full Portland seasons from 1979–87.

Y is for Danny **Y**oung. Young's 1988–92 Portland career coincided with one of the team's most legendary eras. While this reserve guard's basketball IQ made him a valuable role player, his most legendary moment might be his barely late buzzer-beater in Game 4 of the 1990 Finals.

Z is for **Z**ach Randolph. This legendary lefty was part of the rough and rowdy Jail Blazers era of the 2000s. But after his 2003 playoff breakout, Randolph used his strength and crafty post moves to become the first Portland player to lead the team in scoring and rebounding in four straight seasons.

The ever-expanding legendary library

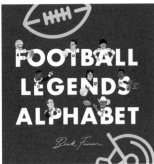

EXPLORE THESE LEGENDARY ALPHABETS & MORE AT WWW.ALPHABETLEGENDS.COM

TRAILBLAZERS LEGENDS ALPHABET

www.alphabetlegends.com

Published by Alphabet Legends Pty Ltd in 2023
Created by Beck Feiner
Copyright © Alphabet Legends Pty Ltd 2023

Printed and bound in China.

9780645851496